THE
KNITTING BRIGADES
OF WORLD WAR I

Volunteers for Victory in
America and Abroad

Holly Korda, Ph.D.

THE KNITTING BRIGADES OF WORLD WAR I: VOLUNTEERS FOR
VICTORY IN AMERICA AND ABROAD

ISBN: 978-0-578-50172-7

Book and cover design by Sarah E. Holroyd
(https://sleepingcatbooks.com)

CONTENTS

INTRODUCTION

In the summer of 1917, following the U.S. entry into the Great War that erupted in Europe in 1914, volunteers from every state, led by the Red Cross, stepped up to knit more than 15 million pounds of wool into socks, sweaters, hats, and bandages for our soldiers and allies overseas. In less than two years, women, men, and the nation's school children knit and purled more than 24 million articles and prepared more than 300 million surgical dressings for U.S. soldiers and allies overseas. The Navy League Comforts Committee added to these unprecedented efforts, along with other voluntary organizations and individuals. These are the Knitting Brigades of World War I, who helped Americans understand who we could be together to unify the nation and support the war effort abroad. This is their story.

A prolific knitter throughout her life, my grandmother, Ruth Warren Webb, was well known for the many mittens, hats, and sweaters she knit for family and friends, church fairs, and community events. She was always busy with a new project and could be found, unfailingly, with knitting needles and yarn in hand.

It was not until I was in my 30s that I happened to ask, "Who taught you to knit?" I expected to hear a story of how her mother or one of her sisters in Chester, Pennsylvania had passed along the skills she had honed throughout her lifetime. Rather, she pulled herself up straight and proudly recounted, "I learned in school when I was 11 years old. The Red Cross came to the school and taught us all to knit—the boys, too. We knit for the war, World War I (1917–18). Bandages from white floss, sweaters without arms, and socks . . . lots of socks for the soldiers. School children like us from every state joined with the adults to do our part for the war."

I was taken aback and fascinated as she shared her memories. Why had I not heard of this before? I had to learn more. So began my journey to discover the amazing efforts of the Knitting Brigades of World War One.

In my search for more information I reached out to the National Red Cross headquarters in Washington, DC, in the mid-1980s. National Historian and Archivist Patrick Gilbo, author of *The American Red Cross: The First Century* (1981), answered my call and graciously offered his knowledge of the WWI knitting efforts along with photocopies of archival materials and old photographs. I will be forever in his debt. I organized the material and provided a brief presentation to staff at the Boston office of the American Red Cross. Like me, they were awed by the amazing story of the knitting brigades and the role of the Red Cross in teaching the nation to knit during WWI.

This story was filed away for several decades before I revisited it a few years ago, now in the Internet Age, to share the story with the community in Maine where I live. Would there be additional photographs and material available online, I wondered? Indeed, I would not be disappointed.

Word spread quickly of this project, leading to invitations to do presentations and talks at libraries and other community gathering spots across the state. I have met knitters, history buffs, and military veterans from more recent wars who have shared their family stories, memorabilia, and knitting tales. All of these experiences have enriched my understanding of the Knitting Brigades and the community of volunteer knitters who continue the tradition by producing knit goods for their local schools, food pantries, homeless shelters, church fairs, soldiers, and refugees here in the U.S. and abroad.

Knitting for the troops became a global phenomenon during the Great War, but took on a special significance in the United States. The stories and photographs in this collection documenting the Knitting Brigades of World War I mark the contributions of the American women, children, and men who helped knit and purl our national identity and a victory overseas. Many organizations and individuals were part of our wartime mobilization, including the American Red Cross; the Navy League Comforts Committee; the Girl Scouts, Boy Scouts, and Campfire Girls; the Salvation Army; the Daughters of the American Revolution; as well as church groups, town committees, women's organizations, and more in cities and small towns across the United States. There was a role for everyone who could pick up needles or crank a sock machine. Those who could not knit could contribute money, plant a Victory Garden, or otherwise roll up their sleeves to help. This is their story, and now ours as well.

There are many organizations and individuals active today, many of whom I have met who are waving the banner to keep the legacy of this inspirational part of our history alive. Digital archives and hobbyist blogs available on the Internet provided a wealth of important material. The Library of Congress and the National Archives are rich repositories of photo images and narratives of the home front activities of World War I. The Center for Knit and Crochet, the World War I Museum, and the Smithsonian Museums include collections that keep the home front knitting activities alive in the modern day. Local historical societies and knitting clubs as well as individuals interested in preserving knitting and fiber arts histories or sharing family tales from "back in the day" contributed to this collection as well. You all have my deepest appreciation and thanks.

This collection of vintage photographs tells the story of the Knitting Brigades of World War I.

I

THE GREAT WAR:
1914–1918

How and why did the United States come to engage in the Great War in Europe, and how did knitting become the rallying cry for victory on the home front and abroad?

America before World War I

The years preceding U.S. involvement in the Great War, World War I, were uneventful for America—seemingly calm with a somewhat restless but unfocused undercurrent to the routine of daily life. The U.S. was ending a period of territorial expansion and conservationism. There was growing concern with the consolidation and control of large corporate and banking interests. Labor movements and unions were forming in many areas of the country, and women were organizing for the right to vote. Progressive and conservative ideologies were widely divergent, resulting in the election of Woodrow Wilson, a middle of the road candidate, as President.

Government infrastructure was limited, with churches, voluntary organizations, and communities addressing many of the social and human service activities that

America before WWI
• Population: 103 million (343 million today)
• President Woodrow Wilson (D-NJ)
• Women's Suffrage (voting rights 1920)
• Voluntary Organizations (limited government infrastructure)

are now the responsibility of various federal, state, and local agencies. The American Red Cross, which would rise to prominence during war time, had only 107 chapters and 200,000 members nationwide. It would soon grow rapidly to 3,864 chapters and more than 30 million members.

Americans knew of the Great War in Europe, World War I, and were aware of the considerable casualties and privations suffered by soldiers and civilians overseas since its start in 1914. Many provided support on a small scale, sending clothing and food to assist the Belgians and the French, in particular, who were known to have suffered especially great losses. But even with the large numbers of immigrants from Europe already in the United States, most viewed the war as an overseas problem that did not warrant U.S. involvement.

Woodrow Wilson, 28th President of the United States

Photo source: Library of Congress

The Great War: Europe and America

World War I was an extremely bloody war with huge losses of life that engulfed Europe from 1914–1919. Fought mostly by soldiers in trenches, World War I saw an estimated 10 million military deaths and more than 20 million wounded. While many hoped that World War I would be "the war to end all wars," the concluding peace in fact set the stage for World War II.

Photo source: U.S. Department of Defense Archive

The spark that started World War I was the assassination of Austria's Archduke Franz Ferdinand and his wife Sophie on June 28, 1914 while Ferdinand was visiting the city of Sarajevo in the Austro-Hungarian province of Bosnia-Herzegovina. The assassination was carried out by a Bosnian Serb nationalist seeking to end Austro-Hungarian rule of the region. Subsequent events resulted in Austro-Hungary declaring war and triggering responses that soon embroiled most of the nations throughout Europe as well as Russia.

Brutal fighting progressed on European soil from 1914, with the United States maintaining a non-interventionist position.

Two major events were soon to unfold, changing American public opinion about the war. The first occurred in 1915, when a German U-boat (submarine) sunk the British ocean liner RMS Lusitania off the coast of Ireland. The Lusitania, like many commercial vessels of the day, carried not only passengers but munitions as cargo. Americans considered the ship to be neutral, as it carried mostly passengers, and were outraged when the Germans sank it, especially since 159 of the passengers were Americans.

The second was the Zimmermann Telegram. In early 1917, Germany sent Mexico a coded message promising portions of U.S. land (AZ, NM, TX) in return for Mexico joining the war against the United States. Britain intercepted and translated the message, and shared it with the United States. Bringing the war to American soil, the U.S. now had a real reason to enter the war on the side of the Allies.

On April 6, 1917, the United States officially declared war on Germany.

The Lusitania

Photo source: Detroit Publishing Company, 1907

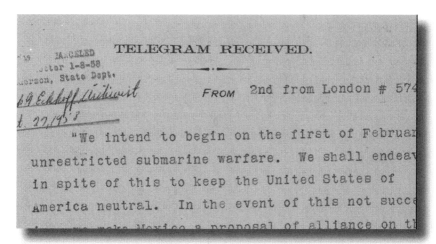

Zimmerman Telegram receipt

Photo source: National Archives

2

RAMPING UP FOR WAR

"It is not an army that we must shape for war, it is a nation."
President Woodrow Wilson

President Woodrow Wilson had committed U.S. troops to the front reluctantly. Public sentiment was divided about intervening in the European war, and the U.S. was ill-prepared for military intervention. Resources were limited, with no infrastructure or financial means to provide even the basics to clothe and feed a civilian military. Public engagement and support at all levels would be essential to meet this commitment, and volunteers would be needed on the home front as well as on the battlefields abroad.

Wilson called on John Joseph "Black Jack" Pershing, a General from Missouri, to head the American Expeditionary Force on the Western Front. A West Point graduate and instructor with a distinguished military career, Pershing had participated in various Indian campaigns and served in the Spanish-American and Philippine-American wars. At Pershing's insistence U.S. forces would serve under his command as a single unit and would not integrate with allied forces.

General John J. Pershing, Commander in Chief of the American Expeditionary Forces. Photo source: Library of Congress

On May 10, 1917, a few weeks after declaring war, President Wilson created a seven-member War Council to oversee war efforts. Among a small number of organizations with national reach and a mission for humanitarian service, the American Red Cross was designated as an arm of government under the leadership of the Council. Wilson appointed Henry P. Davison, a prominent member of J.P. Morgan and Company, as Chair. Other members were from the private sector as well.

President Woodrow Wilson with the original World War I American Red Cross War Council, 1917

Front row (left to right): Robert W. DeForest (not a member), President Wilson, former President William Howard Taft, Eliot Wadsworth. Back row (left to right): Harry Davison, Col. Grayson M.P. Murphy, Charles D. Norton, Edward N. Hurley. Cornelius Bliss, a member, is not pictured. George Case, not pictured, was appointed a member by President Wilson in early 1918, succeeding Norton.

Photo source: Harris & Amp Ewing/National Geographic Society/ CORBIS

The new War Council replaced the existing Executive Committee of the Red Cross. Davison and his council members immediately set out to identify key tasks for the war and put into place a strategy to extend the reach of the Red Cross from the 555 chapters reported in

April 1917 to what would become an impressive 3874 chapters by 1919. This strategy would prove a model for extending the reach of the Red Cross and other national organizations in future years.

> The country was mapped out into four divisions, each with a director in charge, and under these were 114 field agents and an office force that grew to more than 300 members. (Davison, p. 10)

The War Council developed close cooperation with the Navy, a partnership that would extend to the volunteer knitting these organizations were soon to get underway as American women, men, and school children joined with knitters in Britain, Canada, and Australia in support of the troops and families impacted by the Great War.

At its first meeting the War Council reached out to General Pershing to see how the Red Cross could best support his efforts on the battlefront. Pershing responded by telegram:

> If you want to do something for me for God's sake 'buck up the French.' They have been fighting for three years and are getting ready for their fourth winter. They have borne a tremendous burden, and whatever assistance we can lend them promptly will be of the greatest possible value. (Davison, p. 13)

Financing would be needed to support wartime activities at home and abroad. The Secretary of the Treasury, William Gibbs McAdoo (Wilson's son-in-law), responded with hopes of creating a broad market for government bonds, called Liberty Loans. The Liberty Loans were developed by the National War Finance Committee, headed by Cleveland H. Dodge of New York, who was charged to raise $100 million.

McAdoo called on everyone from Wall Street bankers to the Boy Scouts to volunteer for campaigns to sell the bonds. He helped recruit the nation's best known artists to draw posters depicting how buying bonds would contribute to the war effort, and he organized giant bond rallies featuring Hollywood stars such as Douglas Fairbanks, Mary Pickford, and Charlie Chaplin.

Liberty Loans

There were four issues of Liberty Loans:
- April 24, 1917 Emergency Loan Act authorizes issue of $5 billion in bonds at 3.5 percent.
- October 1, 1917 Second Liberty Loan offers $3 billion in bonds at 3 percent.
- April 5, 1918 Third Liberty Loan offers $3 billion in bonds at 4.5 percent.
- September 28, 1918 Fourth Liberty Loan offers $6 billion in bonds at 4.25 percent.

Interest on up to $30,000 in the bonds was tax exempt.

These war bonds were promoted widely as a patriotic duty.

Photo source: S.H. Riesenberg, Smithsonian American Art Museum

Photo source: National Archives

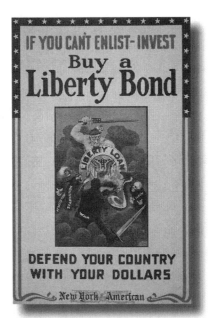

Photo source: W. McKay,
Library of Congress

Mrs. Mabel Thorp Boardman, uncropped photo by Harris & Ewing, American Red Cross Collection.

Photo source: Harris & Ewing, American Red Cross Collection, Courtesy of The American National Red Cross. All rights reserved in all countries.

Women had played important roles in the Red Cross's humanitarian work although they were restricted from management positions, which were held by men. Among the organization's most notable contributors was Mrs. Mabel Thorp Boardman, a philanthropist and socialite from Cleveland who had been active recruiting nurses and securing the organization's finances. She has been described as the effective head of the American Red Cross when the organization was re-chartered in 1904 and became the only woman on the Red Cross Central Commission, the organization's driving force. In keeping with the times, Boardman refused the position of Chair for fear the Red Cross would not be credible to the public with a woman at the helm.

With President Wilson's creation of the War Council, an all-male group composed of bankers and lawyers, Boardman's role was marginalized. She quickly regrouped, however, and formed the Women's Advisory Committee in 1917. The new Committee coordinated volunteer activities for American women who wanted to do their part for the war effort.

Boardman set forth to make sure these priorities were met. She took inventory of what was needed. Garments for soldiers were quickly identified as a priority to address the winter cold. Socks were especially important due to widespread problems caused by trench foot, a fungal condition that led to gangrene and amputations. The most effective solution to trench foot was changing socks frequently to keep feet dry. Bandages and hospital garments were also priority needs. U.S. manufacturers were overwhelmed and unable to supply these demands.

Boardman turned to hand knitters for help and then set about organizing women, children, and even men in every state of the country to knit for the war. The country was organized first by region, then by state and within each state schools, churches, town facilities, and private residences were transformed to play a role coordinating knitting efforts for the war.

Miss Florence Marshall, formerly Director of the Manhattan Trade School, the largest technical school for girls in America, was appointed Director of a newly formed Women's Bureau of the Red Cross in 1917. In her new role, Miss Marshall established many of the standards and logistics for knitting and other garments. One of her first activities was to send two representatives to France and England to consult with authorities about items needed. She then turned her focus to manufacturing large quantities of items, and to standardizing their production so that goods produced by volunteers in regions across the U.S. would be uniform in size and shape. Marshall issued 500,000 flyers with knitting instructions for priority garments, and worked with the Supply Service of the Red Cross and the Bureau of Standards to obtain large quantities of knitting needles and yarn in khaki, blue, and gray. (Clarke, Ida, Ch. 11).

3

CALLING ALL VOLUNTEERS

Widespread public recruitment campaigns were set in motion and swept the nation. Poster art became a leading form of wartime "propaganda" calling the nation to action.

"Uncle Sam" became the ambassador of World War I recruitment. The iconic image was created by James Montgomery Flagg, an American artist who copied the popular image of Britain's Lord Horatio Herbert Kitchener, Secretary of State for War in WWI

Photo source: Library of Congress

Britain. Flagg imposed his own face on Uncle Sam, presenting a take charge leader for the American poster.

Uncle Sam recruitment poster, 1917   Red Cross recruitment poster

Photo source: James Montgomery   Photo source: Library of Congress
Flagg, Library of Congress

Spreading a wide net, the Red Cross, Navy League, and other organizations pulled everyone into the war effort.

Dogs played an important role in the German and Allied military efforts. Dogs were not used widely in the U.S. military until World War II but did serve as mascots and companions for the troops.

Photo source: Mildred Moody, Pritzker Military Museum

Overnight, the nation was transformed in an unprecedented effort. Thousands of new volunteers joined the cause—sewing, knitting, making bandages. Davison later wrote, "It was the age of wool; everybody was knitting."

You Can Help—American Red Cross poster

Photo source: W.T. Benda, Library of Congress

The Greatest Mother in the World—American Red Cross

Photo source: A. E. Foringer, Library of Congress

More than 15 million pounds of wool were worked into garments and bandages by volunteers of "The Great Mother," as the Red Cross came to be known.

When women knit, they knit necessities: 24 million articles for soldiers and sailors, 14 million items of hospital supplies, 6 million refugee garments, and some 300 million surgical dressings. Items included scarves, hats, socks, sweaters, and more.

As the war progressed there would be a shortage of yarn—and people would scorn anyone who might knit for themselves when needs abroad were so great.

Sheep grazing on the White House lawn during WWI.

Photo source: White House Historical Association

As a symbol of home front support to the troops overseas, President Woodrow Wilson had a flock of 48 sheep grazing on the White House lawn, saving manpower by cutting the grass.

President Wilson's personal physician, Navy Surgeon Admiral Cary T. Grayson, was designated the "shepherd of the flock," charged with overseeing the White House sheep. Grayson was not pleased but stepped up to the role. When it came time to shear the flock, President Wilson directed Grayson to send 2 pounds of the 100 pounds of wool produced to every state to be auctioned for the war effort, raising $52,823 for the Red Cross. Grayson would later be designated Chairman of the Red Cross.

4

THE SPIRIT OF AMERICA

Our Boys Need Sox—Knit Your Bit Red Cross recruitment poster showing a basket of yarn and knitting needles, ca. 1914–1918.

Photo source: Library of Congress

Knitting was already a popular past time for women around the time of World War I but the call for home front support pushed this interest into high gear. Everyone was knitting—women, men, children in schools.

Knitting became a social rite as women gathered for knitting teas, carrying patriotic knitting bags in red, white, and blue for their yarn and needles. Knitting skirts with large pockets for supplies became fashionable. Music was often played and sung at these gatherings, featuring songs like "I Wonder Who's Knitting for Me," "Every Girl is Knitting," "Every Stitch is a Thought of You, Dear," and others.

 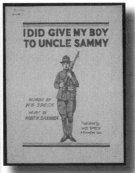 

Women were careful not to be seen knitting for themselves or their families; all available yarn was to be used for war-related knitting. In fact, it was common to see knitters in church, at dinner parties, and the theater, at any available break or free time.

"WOOL WILL WIN THE WAR—DON'T WEAR IT,"

fast became the slogan of the day.

And Then She'd Knit, Knit, Knit
Henry Von Tilzer Music Publishing Co., 1917
Lyrics: Eddie Moran   Music: Harry Von Tilzer

Pretty little Kitty's got the patriotic craze
Knitting scarfs for soldiers day and night.
Billy little Billy now is spending all his days
Watching Kitty knit with all her might.
She even knits while out in his canoe.
She knits while Billy tries to bill and coo.
He'd take a hug then he'd hug her some more
While she'd knit knit knit knit knit.
He'd steal a kiss then he'd take an encore
And she'd knit knit knit knit knit.
Under a tree he would rest with a smile
She'd lay her knitting down just for a while.
A bird in a nest said oh give us a rest
Go on and knit knit knit.

Pretty little Kitty said, now Willie do your bit
Here's some yarn and needles you can start
Come and sit by me and I'll teach you how to knit
That's the way that you can win my heart.
He'd knit a while and then he'd want to woo.
He'd look at her and drop a stitch or two
He'd take a hug then he'd hug her some more
She'd say knit knit knit knit knit.
One day a tug passed by in a squall
Looking through glasses was captain and all—
They both heard a yelp—do you need any help—
And she said knit knit knit.

Wealthy supporters including John D. Rockefeller and Mrs. Joseph Pulitzer did their part, opening their homes to volunteers knitting for the war effort. Rockefeller offered space in his New York City mansion to store yarn and other supplies as well.

Women knit at the Red Cross Knitting Booth while waiting for their trains at New York's Grand Central Station, 1918.

Photo source: National Archives

Women knitting, public vocational schools, 1918.

Photo source: Library of Congress

Knitting for the soldiers while waiting to be served.

Photo source: National Archives

U.S. Grand Jury knitting socks with women for soldiers, Seattle, Washington.

Photo source: National Archives

One of the first business organizations in New York, and, it is believed, the first in the United States, to encourage knitting among its male employees during lunch hour, was the Universal Motion Picture Company, 1600 Broadway, New York. The female stenographers acted as instructors. Photo shows a noon hour knitting session in one of the offices.

Photo and caption source: National Archives

Silent film actress Mary Pickford, known as "America's Sweetheart," knitting a sweater for a WW1 veteran, 1925. Pickford actively encouraged Americans to buy Liberty Bonds to support the war.

Photo source: Library of Congress

Mr. J. Leon Phillips holding yarn for his wife as she knits for the war effort in Palm Beach, Florida, 1917.

Photo source: Library of Congress

Woman's National Service School under Woman's Section, Navy League. Knitting, 1918. Women's National Service Schools, established prior to U.S. involvement in WWI, trained women to serve in non-combat roles in the event of war.

Photo and caption source: Library of Congress

Women and girls knitted and rolled bandages for soldiers at a Red Cross workshop, Fort Yates, at the Standing Rock Reservation. The table, boxes on the floor, and the rack behind them are filled with the bandages they rolled and the socks and sweaters they knitted. The people of Standing Rock and other reservations contributed time, labor, and cash to the Red Cross for the war effort. While most Lakotas lived in poverty, they purchased $100,000 in war bonds and contributed $2,000 to the North Dakota Red Cross to fund hospitals overseas, according to the State Historical Society of North Dakota. None of the men from Standing Rock asked for deferments or military service exemptions.

Photo and caption source: Courtesy of State Historical Society of North Dakota, Image 27

Girls knitting at the Whittier School, Hampton, Virginia, 1918.

Photo source: National Archives

School boys at B. F. Day Elementary School, Seattle, Washington, knitting, 1918.

Photo source: Courtesy of Seattle Public School Archives

Many of the wounded knit as they recuperated from their wounds. Recovery was often a long process and knitting provided productive, usually welcome activity.

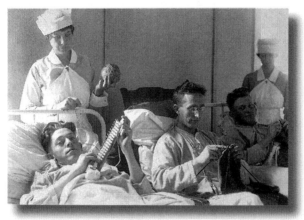

Bed-ridden wounded, knitting. The soldier to the left is using a hand loom. Walter Reed Hospital, Washington, D.C.

Photo source: Harris and Ewing, National Archives

Army soldiers, Walter Reed Hospital, 1918. The soldier to the left is using a circular knitting machine for making socks.

Photo source: Harris and Ewing, National Archives

St. Paul, Minnesota, ca. 1917–1918. A fireman sits on the front of his fire engine, knitting a sock for a soldier in WWI.

Photo source: Minnesota Historical Society

5

THE JUNIOR RED CROSS

Patriotic fervor swept the country and the nation's children were moved to do their part for the war effort like the adults, leading to the formation of the Junior Red Cross. The Junior Red Cross was the idea of Dr. Henry Noble McCracken, President of Vassar College. Members would be organized through the schools in partnership with the Red Cross. During summer breaks schools remained open from three to five days a week for Red Cross work.

Junior Red Cross members were expected to raise funds, make useful items for "suffering children in foreign lands," and help out with things that adult members had no time to do. In fact, these students played a key role shoring up home front readiness; they knit scarves, rolled bandages, and built furniture for health care facilities.

War Council Chairman Davison recalls, "We will let them see democracy at work so that they may know what to do tomorrow." President Wilson made the movement official on September 15, 1917, telling American youth that they could share in "the best work in the great cause of freedom." By February 1919, 12 million youth had paid their 25 cent membership to join the Junior Red Cross.

Mirroring the interest in wearing uniforms, which became the fashion of the day, junior members fashioned their own garments and set to work. The Junior Red Cross contributed $3,677,380 in funds during WWI, and ten percent of all Red Cross products, including knitting.

Girl Scouts, Campfire Girls, and Boy Scouts also stepped up to do their part for the war. Campfire Girls worked at the behest of the Red Cross and other women's groups, while Girl Scouts and Boy Scouts addressed food and garden work to sustain the soldiers. "Every Scout to Feed a Soldier," became the Boy Scouts' rallying cry.

Children knitting for the Junior Red Cross, ca. 1918.
Photo source: Center for Knit and Crochet

Plainfield, NJ school children knitting for the Junior Red Cross, 1917.

Photo source: Library of Congress

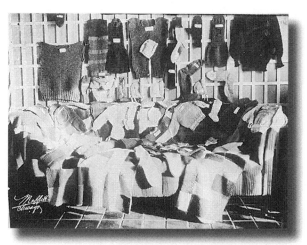

Knitted garments made by the Junior Red Cross, Central Division, Chicago, Illinois. March 1919.

Photo source: Library of Congress

Junior Red Cross members knitting sweaters for the soldiers, New Orleans, 1918.

Photo source: National Archives

Ruth Stevens, age 6 years, Skagway, Bank of Alaska, Piers, 1918.

Photo source: Library of Congress

Knitting was encouraged by multiple campaigns including the American Red Cross's urge to 'knit your bit'. The Navy League also sponsored knitting campaigns including the Central Park Knitting Bee, 1918. Other voluntary organizations participated in the war effort by focusing on specific war-related activities. The Salvation Army became known for its work abroad, including providing doughnuts and other baked goods in France as well as other Allied regions. The YMCA provided programs and services for spiritual support of the troops. Knitting garments and addressing food preservation became the focus of the Daughters of the American Revolution. Local groups and organizations nationwide also stepped up with service in support of the war.

Distributing wool to women knitting for our boys in the U.S. Navy, ca. 1917.

Photo source: Library of Congress

6

CENTRAL PARK
KNITTING BEE

The largest gathering of war time knitters took place in Central Park during a three-day knitting bee over the weekend of July 31, 1918. Headed by the Comforts Committee of the Army and Navy League, the event was created to produce garments for soldiers. A 50 cent entry fee was charged to provide yarn for knitters who could not afford to supply their own.

Several hundred knitters attended, including young and old, men as well as women. Contests were held for the most garments produced, knitting speed, and more. Contestants were awed by the speed of Mrs. Riggs, who completed a sweater in less than seven hours one afternoon, and a later record set by Mrs. Olivia Kindelberger who knit a record ten sweaters in less than seven days. Contests also featured four blind knitters, children under age 11, and an 83-year-old woman. (Macdonald, *No Idle Hands*, Ch. 10)

At the conclusion of this highly successful event, knitters had produced hundreds of sweaters, socks, mufflers, and wristlets. Four thousand dollars was raised in addition to the many garments turned over to the Comforts Committee.

Knitters in the Navy League's Central Park Knitting Bee, 1918.

Photo source: Underwood and Underwood, National Archives

MANY ENTER KNITTING BEE.

Woman of 83 Years Joins Novel Cen al Park Contest.

Several hundred knitters, young and old, men and women, have entered the knitting bee contest under the auspices of the Comforts Committee of the Navy League, Mrs. Herbert L. Satterlee, Chairman, which opens in the Mall at Central Park at 1 P. M. today. One of the contestants for the knitting bee who entered yesterday was Mrs. F. J. Lunaschloss of 371 West 116th Street, who is 83 years old. Mrs. Lunaschloss knits eight hours every day for the soldiers, and says that she is going to keep it up as long as the war lasts.

A contest among six blind women will be one of the features today. The one knitting a four-inch square soonest will win the prize. There will be a knitting machine contest among firemen and Louis Mann and Sam Bernard, co-stars in "Friendly Enemies," who have been practicing for several weeks, to see who can drop the fewest stitches in five minutes.

The New York Times
Published: July 30, 1918
Copyright © The New York Times

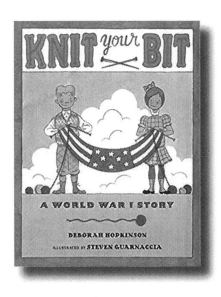

Deborah Hopkinson's 2013 children's book, *Knit Your Bit*, tells the story of the Central Park Knitting Bee.

Central Park knitting bee attendees, including British soldiers and a Civil War veteran, 1918.

Photo source: Library of Congress

Knit Your Bit

Swiftly, to and fro,
      Let your needles fly!
Be not yours to know
      Pause, for tear or sigh.

Stitch by stitch they grow,
      Garments soft and warm
That will keep life's glow
      In some shivering form.

Sweater, muffler, sock,
      For the soldiers' wear!
List to pity's knock –
      For those "over there."

Children's voices, too,
      In the sad refrain,
Wring our hearts anew,
      From that word of pain.

Banish for awhile
      Tints of brighter hue,
Welcome with a smile
      Khaki, gray and blue.

Days are cold and drear,
      Nights are long and bleak,
Thoughts from home are dear,
      Where the cannons shriek.

Let some simple thing,
      That your hand employs,
Cheer and comfort bring
      To our gallant Boys.

May there be no end
      To what love supplies!
Thus their share we'll send
      To our brave Allies!
A.M.D., October, 1917

7

IT TAKES A COMMUNITY

The actual knitting of soldiers' socks, wristlets, and vests was done in cities and towns across the U.S., where local leaders stepped up to store and distribute yarn, knitting needles, and official patterns made available through the American Red Cross. Coordination of activities involved a network of national, state, and community efforts involving schools, churches, as well as other formal and informal groups of knitters.

Grace Walker Campbell (Mrs. Fred Campbell), Warren, Maine.
Photo source: Courtesy of Warren Historical Society

One of many local community leaders who stepped up to help coordinate the Red Cross knitting efforts, Grace W. Campbell, wife of a local physician, Dr. Fred Campbell, and an active member of the Warren Second Congregational Church, kept journals tracking yarn, supplies, and garments produced by community members for U.S. troops overseas. Seventy-four women participated in her local knitting group. She maintained a file of cards and letters from soldiers who gratefully received knitted goods from the community. Volunteer knitters were also known to sometimes include brief notes of encouragement and support to soldiers.

Battery A 319th Field Artillery Camp Gordon Atlanta GA
Dear Mrs. Campbell   Nov 8 1917

Just a line from here in the sunny south I want to thank you for the things you sent me in Camp Devens and I must say though they are woolen I can sure use them here for the nights are cool and they come in fine at night and in the morning as we have to get up at 5:15 here and it is real soupy some mornings you can bet and as to the sweater I wear it nearly all the time. But say this is a queer army they not only don't provide enough clothes but they seem to think we don't need to be payed off no one here have drown any pay yet and no signs of any yet well I must thank you again and close and Remain very grateful,

Frank E Percy

PS Best Regards to Dr. Campbell

Mrs. Grace Campbell Warren Maine
My Dear Mrs. Campbell: October 17 1917
I want to express my sincere thanks through you to the Warren Branch of the American Red Cross for the gift of woolen socks and mittens.

As I have been called to active service I know I shall have many chance to use them this winter and they will be sincerely appreciated.
Very truly yours, Carl D Everingham

Camp Devens   December 16 1917
Dear Madam,

I have received your helmet and was more than pleased with it I thank you
very much for it I received it Saturday noon and I had to go on guard that
very night so it certainly came in handy it will also keep me warm it is very
cold out here just now it's a friend of mine here that told me to write to
Warren Maine and if I did I surely get one so I did. My home is in New
Hampshire but I was sent from Bridgeport Conn to here and the Red Cross
did not furnish me anything the rest of the boys here as all they outfit. This
will be all for now will close by wishing you a Merry Christmas and a happy
New Year with all my heart. We won't be able to go home for Christmas I
don't think because some of the boys here has the measles and they send
them to the hospital.

From a Soldier Boy Wilfed Fournier
B.D 303 H.F.A Camp Devens Mass
PS I was thru the state of Maine quite a lot

Transcription: Karin Larson, Warren Maine Historical Society

Most volunteers used the American style of knitting also referred to
as English knitting. This involves holding the yarn in the right hand
and placing the yarn over the needle to create a stitch. Continental
style knitting, also known as German knitting or left-handed knitting, involves holding the yarn in the left hand and putting the needle through the next stitch to pick the yarn through. Experienced
knitters would sometimes increase their efficiency by using double
knitting techniques that enable production of two socks simultane-
ously on one set of needles.

Sock patterns and styles evolved throughout the war effort. Sock
heels and toes were challenging for many inexperienced knitters,
and sock seams could be uncomfortable for soldiers on the front

University of Washington student Geraldine Gilbert knitting
two socks at once for World War I soldiers, 1918.

Photo source: MOHAI (1983.10.7137.1)

lines. A new technique attributed to Britain's Secretary of State for
War, Horatio Herbert Kitchener, called the "Kitchener Stitch," was
an effort to address this by grafting or weaving two sets of stitches
still on the needle with a tapestry needle. The Red Cross also called
for heel-less hospital socks. Tube socks became popular, especially
among volunteers using sock knitting machines.

The Red Cross distributed knitting patterns that were in turn promoted by local newspapers and women's magazines such as *The
Modern Priscilla* and *Delineator*. Pattern books by yarn manufacturers and others also appeared featuring socks, mufflers, wristlets,
helmets, sweaters and vests. The Red Cross would provide yarn to
knitters, and many who could afford to purchase their own yarn did
so; those who could not knit were encouraged to contribute whatever
funds they could to provide yarn for those who could.

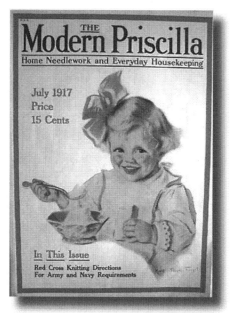

The Modern Priscilla Magazine, July 1917 World War I Issue, out of print.

The Delineator World War I Knitting Patterns, 1917.

WWI Knitting for the Troops, The Priscilla Book of Knitting.

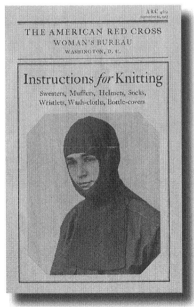

Instructions for Knitting, The American Red Cross.

WWI knit helmets.

Photo source: Smithsonian Museum of American History

WWI wristlet with exposed fingers and thumb for gunners.

Despite the volunteers' best intentions, some
knit items sent to soldiers were misshapen and
the butt of jokes—though gratefully received.
This cartoon, drawn by Albian Wallgren, was
published in the March 8, 1918 edition of the
"Stars and Stripes."

8

Tools for Home Front Knitters

Sioux Indian boys making needles for the Red Cross, South Dakota, ca. 1918.

Photo source: Marquette University at the Center for Knitting and Crochet

Volunteers used a combination of hand knitting needles, hand looms, and circular sock knitting machines to produce socks and other knitted goods for the war. However, most items were knit on traditional needles made of steel or wood.

Gearhart circular sock knitting machine.

The nation's yarn manufacturers went into overdrive to produce skeins for volunteers who knit or used hand looms or sock machines. Manufacturers included Bear Brand, Fleischer, Eskimo, and others. Some yarn was imported from abroad when supplies ran short.

> In September 1918, all American yarn retailers were ordered by the War Industries Board to turn over their stock of service yarn (any yarn in khaki, gray, heather, natural, or white) to the Red Cross. For the next six weeks all yarn for war effort knitting was available only through the Red Cross. This was done to ease the yarn shortage and to allow Red Cross knitting to continue uninterrupted.
>
> Paula Becker, *Knitting for Victory – World War I*

Garfield Worsted Mills Yarn Dyeing Department, Garfield, New Jersey, ca. 1918.

Photo source: National Archives

American Red Cross Workers using knitting machines, 1918.

Photo source: National Archives

Five knitting machines were installed at N.Y. University. These machines knit three socks per hour.

Photo source: Library of Congress

9

OTHER HOME FRONT EFFORTS

Knitting and rolling bandages as part of the knitting and wool brigades, serving as a nurse, or as a service support worker, were not the only ways American civilians stepped up to support the "Sammies," as American soldiers were called. Women, in particular, faced new opportunities that expanded their roles in the workforce and as home makers. And, while the war had many supporters, it also had opponents who called for peace and non-intervention.

Women in the Workforce

With more than 6 million men, representing every state in the country, having enlisted to fight overseas, many essential jobs were left to be filled here at home. Women took on their roles, with many serving in traditional women's positions as nurses and others joining the workforce as factory and shipyard workers, office staff, and more.

The Suffragette Movement was well underway before the U.S. entered the war, and many seized the war-time opportunities to further their cause. With the demonstration of women's contributions on the home front, President Wilson urged the Senate, in September 1918, to pass the 19th Amendment to allow women the right to vote. The House already had moved women's voting rights forward.

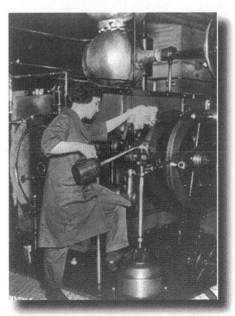

Woman working at the Colt Manufacturing Company during World War I.

Photo source: Library of Congress

Women workers at the Portland Company, Portland, Maine, manufacturing 108mm shell casings, 1918. The Portland Company manufactured tens of thousands of these howitzer shell casings.

Photo source: Collections of the Maine Historical Society, courtesy of Mainememory.net

Patriotic Pageants and Service Clubs

Patriotic fervor fueled many civilian efforts in support of the war. Home service companies, canning clubs, many involving young women and men in hand sewn uniforms, cropped up in small towns to raise funds for the war. These groups planted crops, canned and sold foods, held bake sales, and sold used magazines with proceeds directed to the war effort.

Patriotic pageants which charged admission to audiences became common place on college campuses and in small cities and towns. These events featured young women and men dressed as historical figures, reciting famous speeches and re-enacting events from a glorified past. A primary purpose of these pageants, in addition to raising funds, was to stoke patriotism in support of the war and a unified home front response.

Oshkosh residents staged a patriotic play at the city's Old Masonic Hall during the American involvement in World War I.

Photo source: Courtesy of the Oshkosh Public Museum, Oshkosh, WI. All rights reserved.

Food Conservation

Among the most visible forms of service during World War I were efforts to conserve food to provide for the troops and Allies and avoid rationing at home. This was crucial to the war effort as the German troops had confiscated or destroyed food supplies in Allied territory. President Wilson appointed Herbert Hoover to head the Food Administration and address these issues at home and abroad. Hoover accepted no pay for the position and later wrote that he saw his job as asking people to "Go back to simple food, simple clothes, simple pleasures. Pray hard, work hard, sleep hard and play hard. Do it all courageously and cheerfully." (Hoover memoire, National Archives)

With the help of housewives and children, and a widespread public information campaign, Hoover was able to cut domestic consumption of foods needed overseas, like sugar, wheat, and meat. One important method was to encourage the nation's women and children to plant home Victory Gardens to expand availability of fresh vegetables.

President Woodrow Wilson created the U.S. Food Administration in 1917, naming Herbert Hoover as director. The Food Administration was created as a government entity to replace a voluntary organization.

Photo source: National Archives

"Uncle Sam says - garden to cut food costs. Ask the U.S. Department of Agriculture, Washington, D.C., for a free bulletin on gardening - it's food for thought."

Photo source: A. Hoen & Co., Library of Congress

10

An Ending—and a Beginning

On November 11, 1918, World War I drew to a close, marked by an armistice that ended fighting on land, sea, and air between the Allies and their opponent, Germany. One of the bloodiest wars in human history, World War I left 10 million military deaths, 6 million civilian deaths, and more than 20 million wounded.

Supporting the troops on the U.S. home front, a new generation of knitters had been born. In the United States alone volunteer knitters—the Knitting Brigades—made more than 24 million military garments and 6.5 million refugee garments. These knitters also made more than 300 million surgical dressings. Many of these efforts were organized by the American Red Cross and the Navy League, but the knitting that became the passion of a patriotic nation was accomplished by women, children, and men representing communities and cities nationwide.

A new nation of American citizens and a national infrastructure for services and supports also emerged from World War I. No longer were people Italians, Irish, Japanese, African and more in America. World War I united all as Americans, pulling together for the troops. Women also gained rights to vote, joining men in this right of citizenship, as Women's suffrage was granted nationally shortly after the war, in 1920.

The post-WWI era was not to be without challenges on the home front. The American Red Cross, which saw its membership increase from 200,000 to over 30 million nationwide during the two years of World War I, again mobilized as the 1918–1919 influenza pandemic swept the country. The Red Cross was quickly drawn to the front lines coordinating nursing; producing and procuring medical supplies and food; transporting patients, health workers, and bodies; and aiding patients' families. It is estimated that one fifth of the world's population was afflicted by influenza including 25 percent of the U.S. population. Many deaths occurred as a result.

The 1920s ushered in the Stock Market Crash of 1929 and the Great Depression, the effects of which were felt through the 1930s and beyond. The crash was the most devastating stock market decline in the history of the United States.

Then, two decades after World War I, the War to End All Wars, the U.S. was back overseas to join European allies in what was to become the largest armed conflict in global history: World War Two (1939–1945). The U.S. joined this global war, involving six continents, in December 1941 after the Japanese bombed the American fleet at Pearl Harbor, Hawaii. This war resulted in 50 million military and civilian deaths, including those of 6 million Jews.

Once again, the nation's volunteer knitters stepped to the fore. Prepared. And once again they cast stitches to needles for the war effort, following the Red Cross's lead.

Woman Knitting, 1941, Washington, DC.

Photo source: John Vachon, Library of Congress

For the volunteer knitters, with appreciation.

RESOURCES

Online

Becker, Paula, *Knitting for Victory—World War I*, History Link Essay 5721, Posted 8/17/2004.
http://www.historylink.org/File/5721

Burgess, Anika. Atlas Obscura, *The Wool Brigades of World War I, When Knitting was a Patriotic Duty*, July 26, 2017.
https://www.atlasobscura.com/articles/when-knitting-was-a-patriotic-duty-wwi-homefront-wool-brigades

Clarke, Ida Clyde. *American Women and the World War*. New York and London: D. Appleton and Company, 1918.
https://net.lib.byu.edu/estu/wwi/comment/Clarke/Clarke00TC.htm

Davison, Henry P., Chairman of the War Council of the American Red Cross. *The American Red Cross in the Great War*. New York: The Macmillan Company, 1919.
https://www.questia.com/read/1328844/the-american-red-cross-in-the-great-war

Fisher, Suzanne. "The Technology of Socks in a Time of War," *The Atlantic*, November 7, 2011.

https://www.theatlantic.com/technology/archive/2011/11/the-technology-of-socks-in-a-time-of-war/248006/

Kitchener Stitch, A History, by Merion, July 27, 2014. https://blog.loveknitting.com/kitchener_stitch_a_history/

North Dakota People Living on the Land, State Historical Society of North Dakota. https://www.ndstudies.gov/gr8/

U.S. Knitting Propaganda—WWI, Center for Knit and Crochet, Blog June 5, 2015. http://centerforknitandcrochet.org/u-s-knitting-propaganda-wwi/

"Why did President Woodrow Wilson keep a flock of sheep on the White House lawn?" The White House Historical Association Q&A. https://www.whitehousehistory.org/questions/why-did-president-woodrow-wilson-keep-a-flock-of-sheep-on-the-white-house-lawn

World War I and the American Red Cross. https://www.redcross.org/content/dam/redcross/National/history-wwi.pdf

Books

Gilbo, Patrick F. *The American Red Cross: The First Century*. New York: Harper and Row, 1981.

Macdonald, Anne L. *No Idle Hands: The Social History of American Knitting*. New York: Ballantine Books, 1988.

Strawn, Susan M. *Knitting America: A Glorious Heritage from Warm*

Socks to High Art. St. Paul, MN: Voyageur Press, 2007.

Strawn, Susan M., "American Women and Wartime Hand Knitting, 1750-1950," in *Women and the Material Culture of Needlework and Textiles, 1750-1950*, M. D. Goggon and B. F. Tobin, eds. Routledge Publishers, 2016.

More Information

Audio

Knitting All the Day: Knitting Songs from WWI by Melanie Gall, 2012. Canadian singer Melanie Gall has compiled and performs 14 popular American knitting songs from World War I in this delightful collection. With Erin Craig, piano; Graeme Mellway, percussion; and Karen Gall, spoken voice.

Books

Davison, Henry P. *The American Red Cross in the Great War*. New York: The Macmillan Company, 1919. Davison, Chairman of the War Council of the American Red Cross, reports on his tenure with the organization in this historic account of Red Cross activities during World War I. Davison provides some information on knitting on the home front and provides detailed accounts of the Red Cross and its role during the war.

Gilbo, Patrick F. *The American Red Cross: The First Century*. New York: Harper and Row, 1981. A richly illustrated volume of photographs and narrative describing the first century of the American Red Cross and its work, by Red Cross historian Gilbo, who so generously shared his research into the knitting brigades as I began my own research years ago.

Macdonald, Anne L. *No Idle Hands: The Social History of American Knitting.* New York: Ballantine Books, 1988. A classic resource on American knitting in its social context, the author has carefully researched this wonderful volume of well documented material about knitting during World War I and in the eras before and after.

Strawn, Susan M. *Knitting America: A Glorious Heritage from Warm Socks to High Art.* St. Paul, MN: Voyageur Press, 2007. This book is a treasure for those interested in the history of knitting in the United States. Author Strawn includes some background on knitting during World War I as well as knitting throughout other periods of the American experience.

Organizations

American Red Cross. The Red Cross has available several online resources documenting the knitting efforts it coordinated as well as the health and medical support it provided through its nursing and volunteer corps during World War I. http://www.redcross.org

Center for Knit and Crochet Digital Repository. Incorporated in December 2012 in Wisconsin to "preserve and promote the art, craft, and scholarship of knitting, crochet, and related arts," this online collection includes items on World War I knitting in the United States and abroad. It includes digital photos and narratives that bring together a global community of individuals, institutions, artists, and collectors. http://www.centerforknitandcrochet.org

Library of Congress. The largest research library in the world, the Library of Congress maintains several digital collections with pho-tographs, images, and narratives describing World War I heroics on the home front and abroad. Many of the photos in this book are the result of my work with their collections. https://loc.gov

National Archives. This government resource maintains various digital data bases, records, photographs and documents that provide another rich source of information on home front activities during World War I. These resources also contributed to this collection. https://archives.gov/research

National Museum of American History. A Smithsonian museum located in Washington, DC, this national treasure contains historical objects and documents that explore the American identity. It has numerous online collections as well. https://www.si.edu/collections

National World War I Museum and Memorial. Located in Kansas City, MO, this organization is America's official World War I museum and memorial. Its physical location houses the world's largest collection of World War I objects. Many resources are available online. https://www.theworldwar.org

Other

Becker, Paula. *Knitting for Victory—World War I,* History Link Essay 5721, Posted 8/17/2004, http://www.historylink.org/File/5721

Gosling, Lucinda in association with Mary Evans Picture Library. *Knitting for Tommy: Keeping the Great Soldier Warm.* Gloucestershire, England: The History Press, 2014. This delightful, well-illustrated book tells the story of knitters in the U.K., from the British perspective.

Hopkinson, Deborah. *Knit Your Bit: A World War I Story.* New York, NY: G.P. Putnam's Sons, 2013. This children's book, illustrated by Steven Guarnaccia, tells the story of the Central Park Knitting Bee during World War I.

Monroe, Emma Chalmers. *Handbook of Wool Knitting and Crochet*, Illustrated Edition, by Anonymous. Dodo Press, originally published by Needlecraft Publishing Company, Augusta, Maine, 1918. This book is a reprint of a handbook of patterns and techniques for knitting and crochet with illustrations from the era. A fascinating find for knitters!

Image Sources

Images listed in order of appearance:

Chapter 1: The Great War: 1914–1918

Photo source: Library of Congress, Digital ID cph 3f06247

Photo source: http://archive.defense.gov/home/features/2014/0614_WWI/timeline/042614hr.jpg

Photo source: Detroit Publishing Company, 1907; Library of Congress, www.loc.gov/pictures/resource/det.4a15960/

Photo source: General Records of the Department of State, National Archives Identifier, 302022

Chapter 2: Ramping Up for War

Photo source: Library of Congress, LOC 6331254533.jpg

Photo source: Harris & Amp Ewing/National Geographic Society/CORBIS

Photo source: Sidney H. Riesenberg, Smithsonian American Art Museum, Over the Top for You, 1918, https://americanart.si.edu/exhibitions/posters-WWI

Photo source: National Archives and Records Administration, NARA 512621.jpg

Photo source: Winsor McKay, Library of Congress, http://hdl.loc.gov/loc.pnp/cph.3g09888

Photo source: ID # 10059-006, Mabel Thorp Boardman, uncropped photo by Harris & Ewing, American Red Cross Collection. Courtesy of The American National Red Cross. All rights reserved in all countries

Chapter 3: Calling All Volunteers
Photo source: Library of Congress digital ID cph.3g03858, http://www.loc.gov/pictures/resource/cph.3g03858

Photo source: James Montgomery Flagg, Library of Congress, http://hdl.loc.gov/loc.pnp/ppmsc.03521

Photo source: Library of Congress, https://www.loc.gov/item/00651751

Photo source: Mildred Moody, https://www.pritzkermilitary.org/explore/museum/digital-collection/view/oclc/10599824

Photo source: W. T. Benda, Library of Congress, https://lccn.loc.gov/2002708897

Photo source: A.E. Foringer, Library of Congress, https://www.loc.gov/pictures/item/2001700434/

Photo source: https://fthmb.tqn.com/a6zKakLJR-

po8G5m61bN-PqtW870=/960x0/filters:no_upscale()/white_house_
sheep-582a5a883df78c6f6a85a075.jpg

Chapter 4: The Spirit of America

Photo source: Library of Congress, http://www.loc.gov/pictures/
item/00652152/

Music covers: http://threadwinder.info/pubs/hist/sheet-
music/WWI/Wonder.htm, https://www.loc.gov/resource/
ihas.200199093.0/?sp=1, http://threadwinder.info/pubs/hist/sheet-
music/WWI/ThenShedKnit.htm

Photo source: National Archives/20802094

Photo source: Library of Congress, https://www.loc.gov/
item/2016819566/

Photo source: National Archives, G. E. Mathios, Waterbury,
Connecticut, https://catalog.archives.gov/id/20803258

Photo source: National Archives, https://catalog.archives.gov/
OpaAPI/media/20802186/content/stillpix/165-ww/BOX_35/
FOLDER_B/165-WW-35B-026.jpg

Photo source: New York Herald, from National Archives, https://
catalog.archives.gov/OpaAPI/media/20802092/content/still-
pix/165-ww/BOX_35/FOLDER_A/165-WW-35A-0https://lccn.
loc.gov/201684075680.jpg

Photo source: Library of Congress, https://lccn.loc.gov/2016840756

Photo source: Library of Congress, https://www.loc.gov/item/92522637/

Photo Source: Library of Congress, www.loc.gov/pictures/resource/hec.01918/?co=hec

Photo source and caption: State Historical Society of North Dakota, https://www.ndstudies.gov/gr8/content/unit-iii-waves-development-1861-1920/lesson-4-alliances-and-conflicts/topic-11-great-war-1917-1918/section-4-lakotas-standing-rock-reservation

Photo source: National Archives/ 20802092

Photo source: www.historylink.org/File/5721, Courtesy Seattle Public School Archives (Neg 218-16)

Photo source: Military Health, Harris and Ewing, 165-ww-265 13-17, National Archives

Photo source: Harris and Ewing, National Archives, NARA-45496560.jpg

Photo source: Minnesota Historical Society/CORBIS, https://www.flickr.com/photos/56834589@N00/68000267/in/photostream/

Chapter 5: The Junior Red Cross
Photo source: http://centerforknitandcrochet.org/u-s-knitting-propaganda-wwi/

Photo source: Library of Congress, https://www.loc.gov/resource/anrc.06039/

Photo source: Library of Congress, https://www.loc.gov/item/2017672997/

Photo source: National Archives, https://catalog.archives.gov/OpaAPI/media/20802444/content/stillpix/165-ww/BOX_37/FOLDER_A/165-WW-37A-014.jpg

Photo source: Library of Congress, https://www.loc.gov/resource/anrc.01725/

Photo source: Library of Congress, https://www.loc.gov/item/2017672156/

Chapter 6: Central Park Knitting Bee
Photo source: National Archives 23923649, Underwood and Underwood, 1918

New York Times, July 30, 1918

Deborah Hopkinson's 2013 children's book, Knit Your Bit, tells the story of the Central Park Knitting Bee.

Photo source: Library of Congress/ LC-DIG-ggbain-27377

Chapter 7: It Takes a Community
Photo source: Courtesy of Warren Maine Historical Society

Letters to Grace Campbell, Warren Historical Society

Photo source: Courtesy of Museum of History and Industry, Seattle, WA (1983.10.7137.1)

Photo source: The Modern Priscilla Magazine, July 1917 World War I Issue, out of print

Photo source: https://americanhistory.si.edu/sites/default/files/file-uploader/Delineator_pattern_WWI.jpg

Photo source: https://binged.it/2EYwAOX

Photo source: https://www.mnhs.org/sites/default/files/-paragraphs/image/blog-post/knitting_book.jpg

Photo source: americanhistory.si.edu https://binged.it/2BTgjc0

Photo source: https://prodimage.images-bn.com/pim-ages/2940013831827_p0_v2_s600x595.jpg

Photo source: http://www.usmilitariaforum.com/forums/index.php?/topic/39625-us-army-knit-clothing-from-1911-to-1918/

Chapter 8: Tools for Home Front Knitters
Photo source: Marquette University at Center for Knitting and Crochet, http://cdm16280.contentdm.oclc.org/cdm/ref/collection/p4007coll4/id/1115

Photo source: https://i.pinimg.com/originals/3a/f6/67/3af-66714775d5cfdfcc13081315a8cbb.jpg

Photo source: https://upload.wikimedia.org/wikipedia/com-mons/7/71/Industries_of_War_-_Cloth_-_Garfield_Worsted_Mills_-_CORNER_OF_THE_YARN_DYING_Department_showing_two_yarn_dyeing_attachments_-_NARA_-_31487618.jpg

Photo source: National Archives: https://catalog.archives.gov/
id/20802256

Photo source: Library of Congress, ca.1917, https://www.loc.gov/
item/2017672021/

Chapter 9: Other Home Front Efforts

Photo source: Library of Congress, https://library.ccsu.edu/dighist-
Fall16/exhibits/show/industry-ct-WWI/item/134

Photo source: Courtesy of Maine Historical Society, http://www.
mainememorynet.item5763

Photo source: Courtesy of the Oshkosh Public Museum, Oshkosh,
WI. All rights reserved.

Photo source: National Archives, National Archives and Records
Administration, Identifier: 512498

Photo source: Library of Congress, A. Hoen & Co., Baltimore, ca.
1917-1918, https://www.loc.gov/item/00653180/

Chapter 10: An Ending—And a Beginning

Photo source: Library of Congress, John Vachon, Washington, DC,
1941, https://www.loc.gov/item/2017765570/

About the Author

Holly Korda became fascinated with World War I volunteer knitting when she learned of these home front heroics from a relative. A researcher by training, she reached out to a Red Cross historian in the 1980s to uncover more about these amazing efforts. Fast forward to the Internet Era, Holly expanded her research on the knitting brigades and has shared numerous presentations on the subject with volunteer knitting groups, veterans, and history buffs.

She is involved with and honors community initiatives that demonstrate the power of the human spirit. A resident of Southern Maine, Holly received her Ph.D. from Tufts University.

Made in the USA
Middletown, DE
09 February 2020

84462313R00057